WAY

Ichthyosaurus

by Daniel Cohen

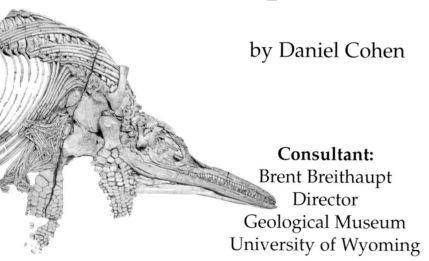

Consultant:
Brent Breithaupt
Director
Geological Museum
University of Wyoming

Bridgestone Books
an imprint of Capstone Press
Mankato, Minnesota

Bridgestone Books are published by Capstone Press
151 Good Counsel Drive, P.O. Box 669, Mankato, Minnesota 56002
http://www.capstone-press.com

Library of Congress Cataloging-in-Publication Data
Cohen, Daniel, 1936–
    Ichthyosaurus / by Daniel Cohen.
        v. cm.—(Discovering dinosaurs)
    Includes bibliographical references and index.
    Contents: Ichthyosaurus—The world of ichthyosaurus—Parts of ichthyosaurus—What
ichthyosaurus ate—Plesiosaurs and Mosasaurs—Live young—End of ichthyosaurus—
Discovery of ichthyosaurus—Studying ichthyosaurus today—Hands on : making imprints—
Words to know.
    ISBN 0-7368-1622-4 (hardcover)
    1. Ichthyosaurus—Juvenile literature. [1. Ichthyosaurus. 2. Prehistoric animals.] I. Title.
QE862.I2 C64 2003
567.9′37—dc21
                                                                            2002011103

Summary: Describes what is known of the physical characteristics, behavior, and habitat
of this reptile that lived during the time of the dinosaurs.

Editorial Credits
Erika Shores, editor; Karen Risch, product planning editor; Linda Clavel, series designer;
    Patrick D. Dentinger, cover production designer; Angi Gahler, production artist;
    Alta Schaffer, photo researcher

Photo Credits
Corbis/Jonathan Blair, 20
The Natural History Museum, 6, 8–9; J. Sibbick, 10, 14
Natural Visions/Heather Angel, cover, 1
Visuals Unlimited/A.J. Copley, 4, 12, 16

1 2 3 4 5 6 08 07 06 05 04 03

Table of Contents

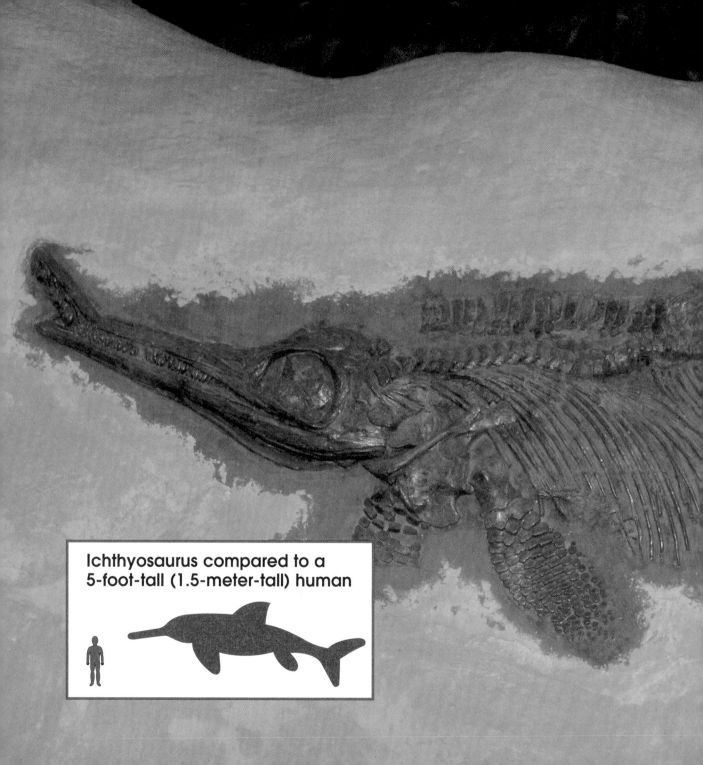

Ichthyosaurus compared to a 5-foot-tall (1.5-meter-tall) human

Ichthyosaurus

Ichthyosaurus (IK-thee-oh-SORE-us) was a reptile that lived from 206 to 140 million years ago. Ichthyosaurus belonged to a group of reptiles called ichthyosaurs. These reptiles were not dinosaurs. But dinosaurs lived during the time of ichthyosaurs.

The World of Ichythosaurus

Water covered much more of the Earth during the time of Ichthyosaurus than today. Ichthyosaurus lived in the ocean. Many kinds of reptiles and fish swam in the ocean with Ichthyosaurus.

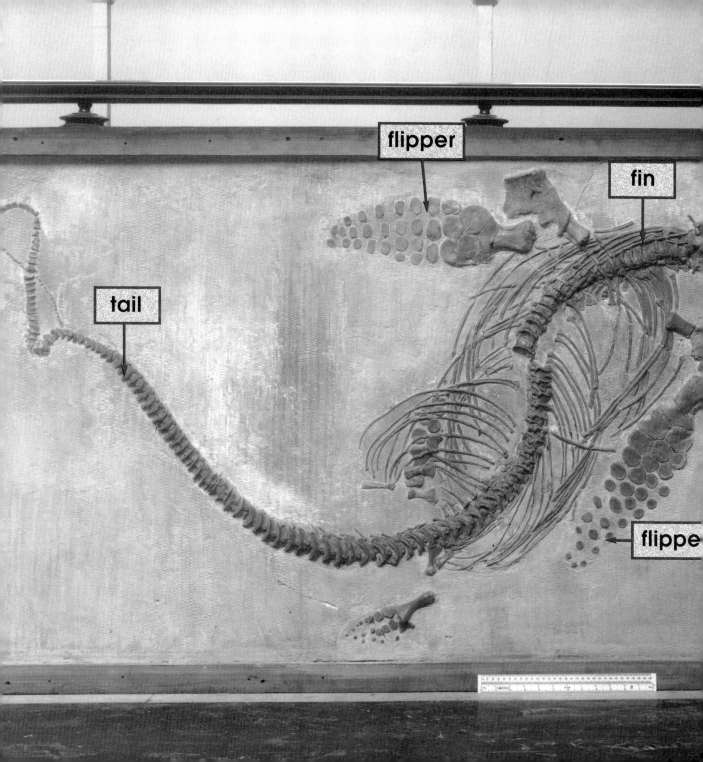

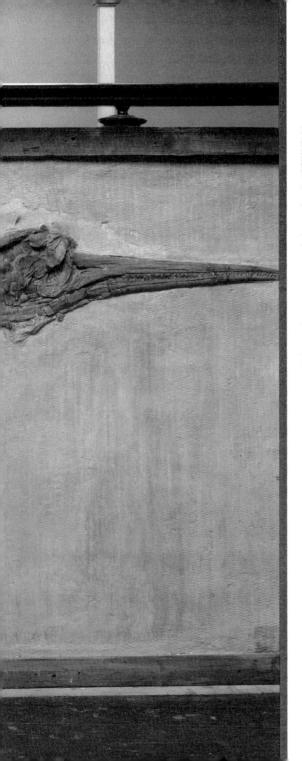

Parts of Ichthyosaurus

Ichthyosaurus means "fish reptile." It looked like a dolphin. Ichthyosaurus had a fin on its back. Its tail ended in a fin. Ichthyosaurus had four powerful flippers on its underside. Ichthyosaurus' flippers and tail helped it swim very quickly.

What Ichthyosaurus Ate

Ichthyosaurus was a predator. It ate other animals. Scientists think Ichthyosaurus ate shellfish, fish, and squid.

plesiosaur

Plesiosaurs and Mosasaurs

Other large reptiles lived in the ocean during the time of ichthyosaurs. Plesiosaurs (PLEE-see-oh-sores) and mosasaurs (MOES-ah-sores) were predators. Some plesiosaurs had very long necks. Mosasaurs had many sharp teeth and a long tail.

Live Young

Most reptiles lay eggs. Some paleontologists think Ichthyosaurus did not lay eggs. Instead, Ichthyosaurus gave birth to live young. A newborn Ichthyosaurus could swim on its own.

paleontologist
a scientist who finds and studies fossils

End of Ichthyosaurus

Ichthyosaurus became extinct about 140 million years ago. Dinosaurs became extinct about 65 million years ago. Some scientists think Ichthyosaurus died because the temperature of the oceans changed.

extinct
no longer living anywhere in the world

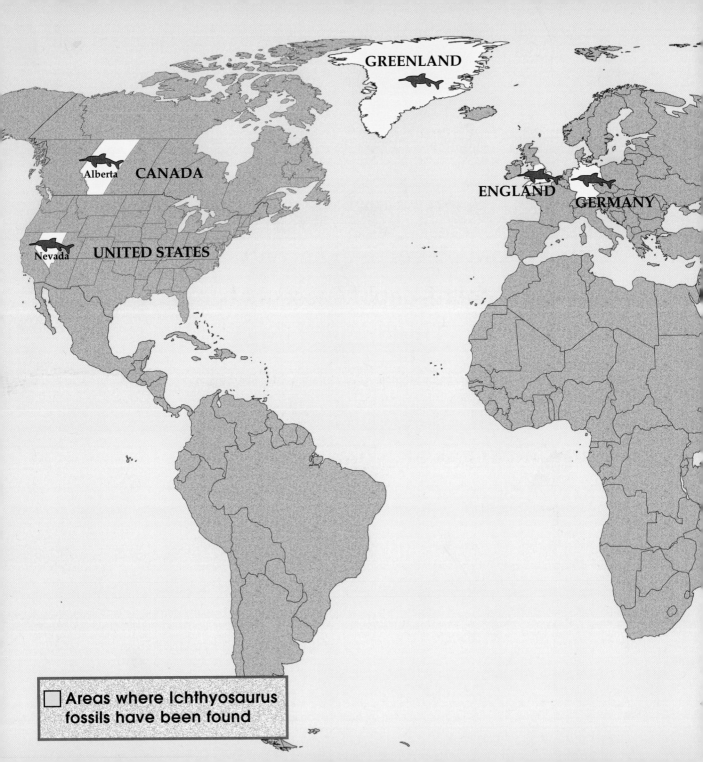

GREENLAND

CANADA

Alberta

UNITED STATES

Nevada

ENGLAND

GERMANY

Areas where Ichthyosaurus
fossils have been found

Discovering Ichthyosaurus

A 12-year-old girl named Mary Anning and her brother Joseph discovered Ichthyosaurus. The Annings lived in Lyme Regis, England. Mary collected fossil shells from the cliffs near her home. In 1811, Mary found the fossil of a 17-foot (5-meter) Ichthyosaurus.

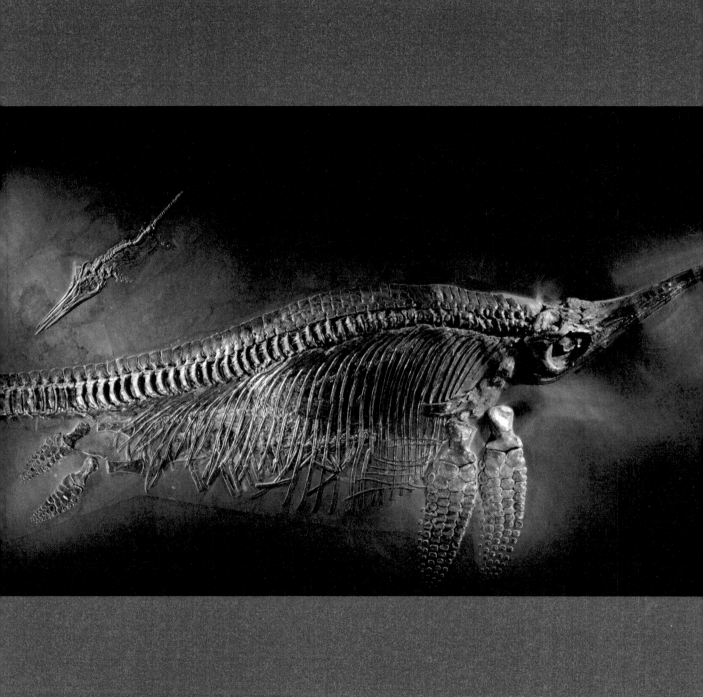

Studying Ichthyosaurus Today

Some fossils of ichthyosaurs were well preserved. These fossils tell paleontologists what Ichthyosaurus and its relatives looked liked when they lived. Some fossils show the shape of Ichthyosaurus' body and fins. Other Ichthyosaurus fossils show what it ate.

Hands On: Making Imprints

Skeletons of Ichthyosaurus often left imprints in rocks. Try this activity to find out what other kinds of material best preserve imprints.

What You Need

Measuring cup   Plastic plates
Small bowl   Shells
Sand   Clay
Water   Gravel
Spoon

What You Do

1. Mix together 1 cup (240 mL) of sand and 1 cup (240 mL) of water in a small bowl. Place the mixture on a plastic plate.
2. Press a few shells into the mixture. Remove the shells. Do the imprints of the shells remain in the mixture?
3. Now try mixing clay and 1 cup (240 mL) of water together. Place the mixture on a plastic plate.
4. Press a few shells into the clay and water mixture. Remove the shells. Can you see the impression the shells made on the mixture?
5. Now put some gravel on a plastic plate. Press some shells into the gravel. Do the shells leave an imprint on the gravel? Which material best preserved the shell impressions?

Words to Know

dinosaur (DYE-na-sore)—an extinct land reptile; dinosaurs lived on Earth for more than 150 million years.

fossil (FOSS-uhl)—the remains or traces of something that once lived; bones and footprints can be fossils.

paleontologist (PAY-lee-on-TOL-ah-jist)—a scientist who finds and studies fossils

predator (PRED-uh-tur)—an animal that hunts and kills other animals for food

preserve (pri-ZURV)—to keep something in its original state

reptile (REP-tile)—a cold-blooded animal with a backbone; scales cover a reptile's body.

scientist (SYE-uhn-tist)—a person who studies the world around us

Read More

Hartzog, Brooke. *Ichthyosaurus and Little Mary Anning.* Dinosaurs and Their Discoverers. New York: PowerKids Press, 1999.

Rodriguez, K. S. *Ichthyosaurus.* Prehistoric Creatures Then and Now. Austin, Texas: Steadwell Books, 2000.

Internet Sites

Track down many sites about Ichthyosaurus. Visit the FACT HOUND at *http://www.facthound.com*

IT IS EASY! IT IS FUN!

1) Go to *http://www.facthound.com*
2) Type in: 0736816224
3) Click on "FETCH IT" and FACT HOUND will find several links hand-picked by our editors.

Relax and let our pal FACT HOUND do the research for you!

Index